Young Learner's

CURSIVE WRITING

CAPITAL LETTERS

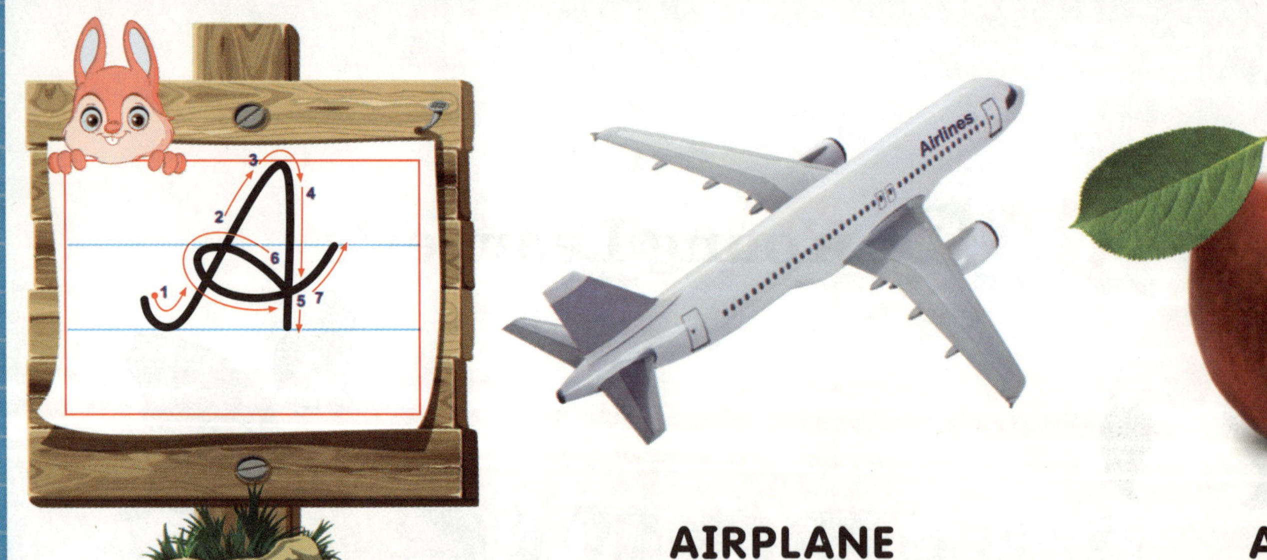

Trace and Practice

BALL

BABY

Trace and Practice

CAT

CRAYONS

Trace and Practice

DATES

DOLL

Trace and Practice

EGGS

ELEPHANT

Trace and Practice

FRUITS

FLOWERS

Trace and Practice

GIFTS

GIRL

Trace and Practice

HAT

HOUSE

Trace and Practice

IRON

ICE CREAM

Trace and Practice

JUG

JEANS

Trace and Practice

KITE

KETTLE

Trace and Practice

LEMONS

LAMP

Trace and Practice

MILK

MONKEY

Trace and Practice

NOTEBOOK

NUTS

Trace and Practice

OLIVES

OCTOPUS

Trace and Practice

PUMPKIN

PENCILS

Trace and Practice

QUAD BIKE

QUILT

Trace and Practice

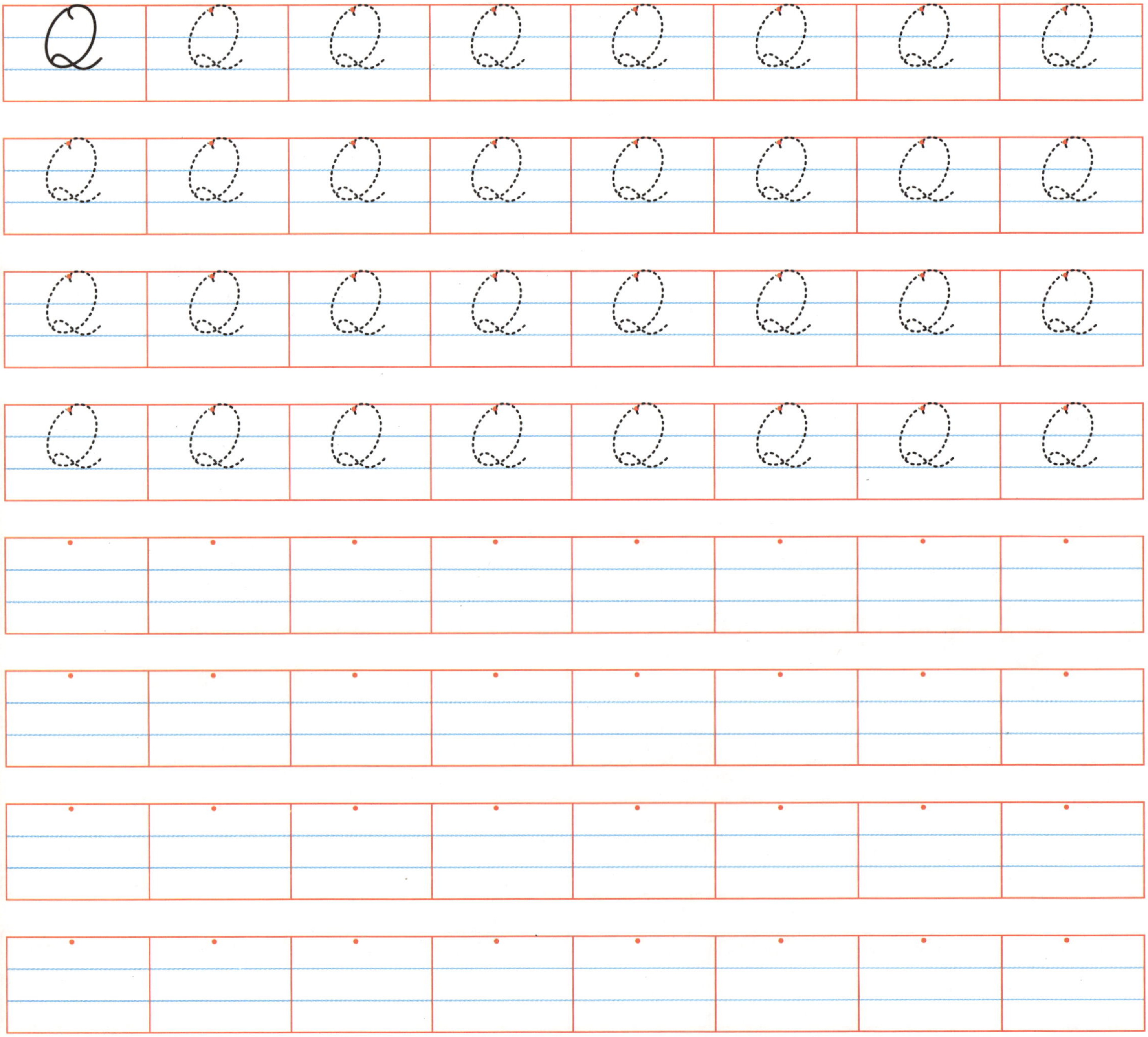

RASPBERRY RIBBON

Trace and Practice

SUGARCANE

SANDCASTLE

Trace and Practice

TOWEL

TELEPHONE

Trace and Practice

T	T	T	T	T	T	T	T
T	T	T	T	T	T	T	T
T	T	T	T	T	T	T	T
T	T	T	T	T	T	T	T

UTENSIL

UMBRELLA

Trace and Practice

VAN

VEGETABLES

Trace and Practice

WATCH

WATERMELON

Trace and Practice

XYLOPHONE

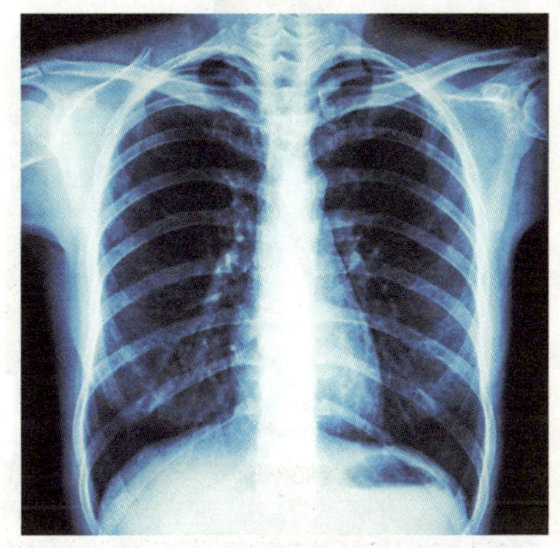

X-RAY

Trace and Practice

YOGURT

YARN

Trace and Practice

ZUCCHINI

ZEBRA

Trace and Practice

Join the alphabet from A to Z to complete the picture.
Now, colour the picture with colours of your choice.

Z Y X U T V S W R Q P K O J L I N M D C H G F E B A

Write the alphabet in cursive with which the name of the object begins.

Match the pictures that begin with the same alphabet.

Write the alphabet in cursive with which the name of the object begins. Now, write the next three alphabet to complete the sequence.

L	*M*	*N*	*O*

Practice writing A to Z